WORLD IN DANGER

# WATER

Steve Pollock
Illustrated by Peter Wingham

Belitha Press

First published in Great Britain in 1990 by
Belitha Press Limited
31 Newington Green, London N16 9PU


Editor: Neil Champion



ISBN 1-85561-032-9

Reprinted 1991, 1992
Printed in Hong Kong for Imago

# Contents

# Water on tap

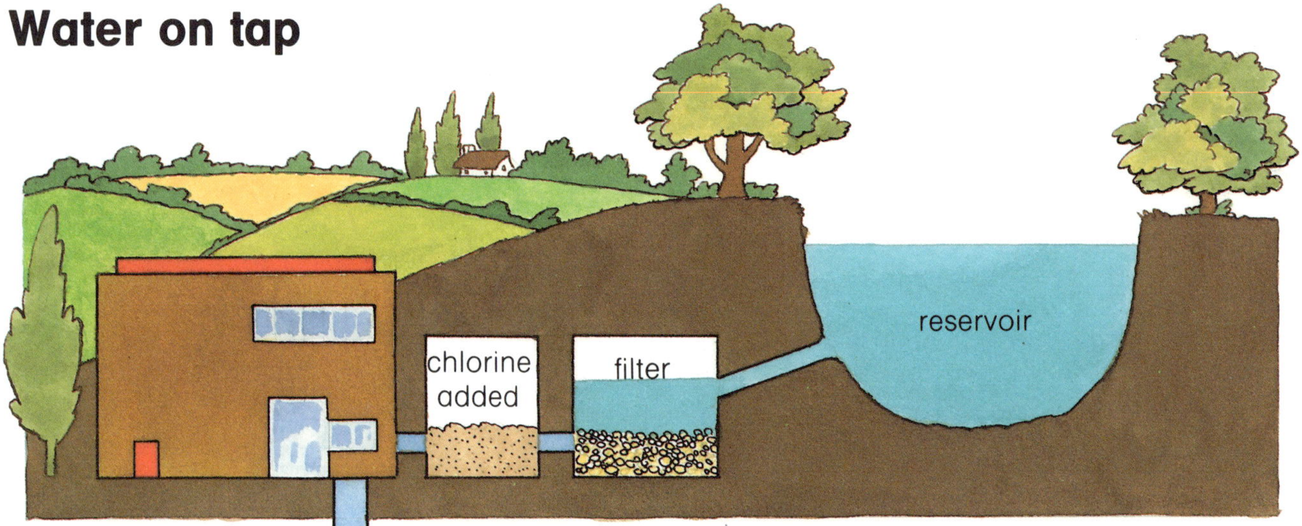


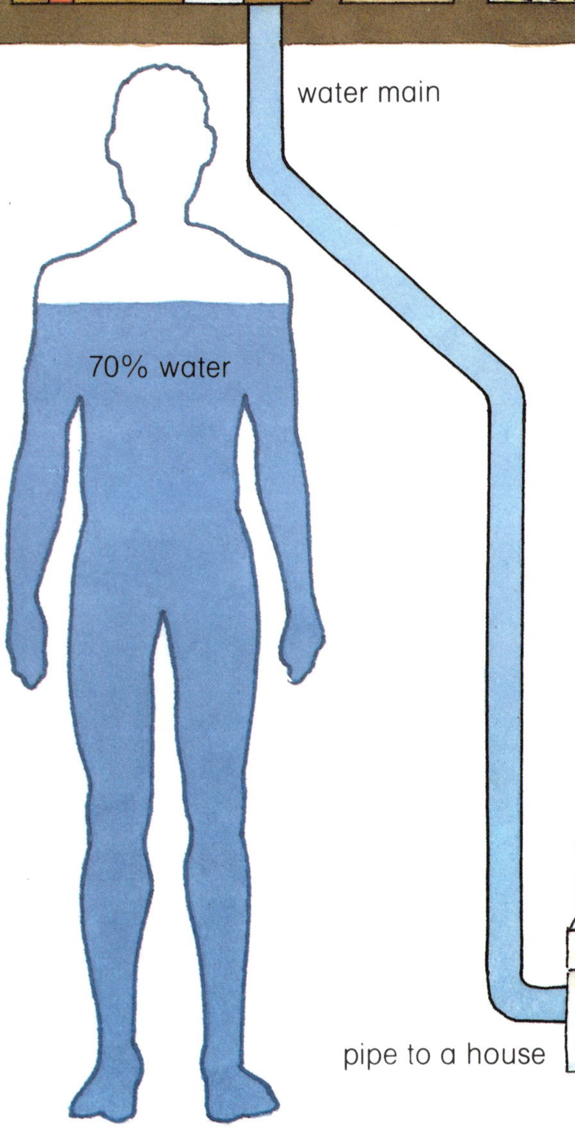


Our bodies are 70% water so we need to drink 5.5 litres every day to stay healthy. The water from taps comes from rivers, lakes or **reservoirs**. It is passed through sand and gravel. This removes germs and tiny plants and animal life.

Sometimes chemicals are added to make the water cleaner. So when we want to drink or wash, pure water comes straight to us from the tap.

Rain falls all over the world and drains deep underground. It passes through soil and many layers of rocks. This removes germs and makes the water clear. If you make a hole deep enough you may reach pure water. When this happens a **well** is made.

Rain does not fall in equal quantities everywhere. For most people in the world, finding clean water for drinking is never easy. They may have to walk several miles to the nearest well.

Wherever you are in the world, water brings great pleasure as well as being important for drinking and washing.

# The water cycle

All over the world, heat from the sun makes water **evaporate** from the sea and rise into the air above us. The water becomes cool again as it rises and makes clouds in the sky. When the clouds pass over mountains, the water in them falls out of the sky as rain.

This rain forms streams. Streams make rivers and then the rivers sometimes make a lake. Eventually, the water makes its way back to the sea and the cycle starts all over again.

# Water pollution

Can you see what's happening here? There are harmful things getting into the water cycle. Smoke from the factory chimneys is going up into the air and chemicals in the smoke mix with rain to make an acid.

This **acid rain** can sometimes make trees in a forest sick. After a time, the trees lose their leaves and die.

Sometimes dangerous chemicals are dumped at sea. Less harmful waste may also be dumped. Although the sea is big, too many chemicals may make plants and animals in the sea more likely to catch diseases. If we eat sick fish, we might be harmed.

# A struggling river

The water in this bowl (**1**) is a little polluted. The water in bowl (**2**) is very polluted. Only those animals which can breathe air such as the Rat Tailed Maggot can survive here.

A clean river (**3**) is full of life. You can find a whole variety of plants and animals living together in a natural balance. That balance can be ruined very quickly by pollution.

**Safety tips**

- Always wash your hands after you have been handling river water.
- Always work at a safe part of the river bank.
- Make sure you go to the river with a grown-up.
- Never eat food until you've washed your hands.

2

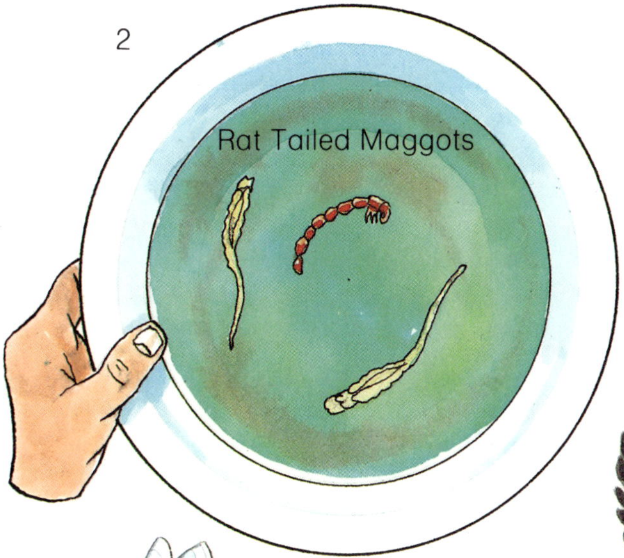


When sewage or waste from a factory gets into the river it begins to rot down. But to rot down all that waste in one go uses a lot of **oxygen** in a very short time. That means there is no oxygen left for living things in the river to breathe.

Those that can, like the frogs, move away. Others, like the insects and fish, may die.

3

# People and pollution

In 1858 the smell of the River Thames was so bad, Members of Parliament left the House of Commons. This led to laws being made which brought in the world's first sewage systems.

In cities all over the world people used to throw their rubbish straight out into the streets. Just walking along the street could be a risky and sometimes very smelly business! This rubbish often ended up in the nearest river or pond.

Today there are **sewage systems** in many parts of the world. Household waste is treated and made safe.

Rivers can also be polluted by chemicals used by farmers. They get into the rivers straight from the land. Sometimes chemicals used to kill pests, such as pesticides, are washed by rain into the river from the fields.

Other chemicals, called **nitrates**, which are used to grow crops can end up there too. The muck from cows and other animals has nitrates in it too. Where there are a lot of cows a river can become polluted with their dung. Life in the river seems to be in a lot of danger!

# Wildlife needs water

One way of controlling a river is to build a **dam** across it. The water can then be used for drinking and irrigation.

Water can also be used to create electricity. Water can be let through the dam to turn a **turbine**.

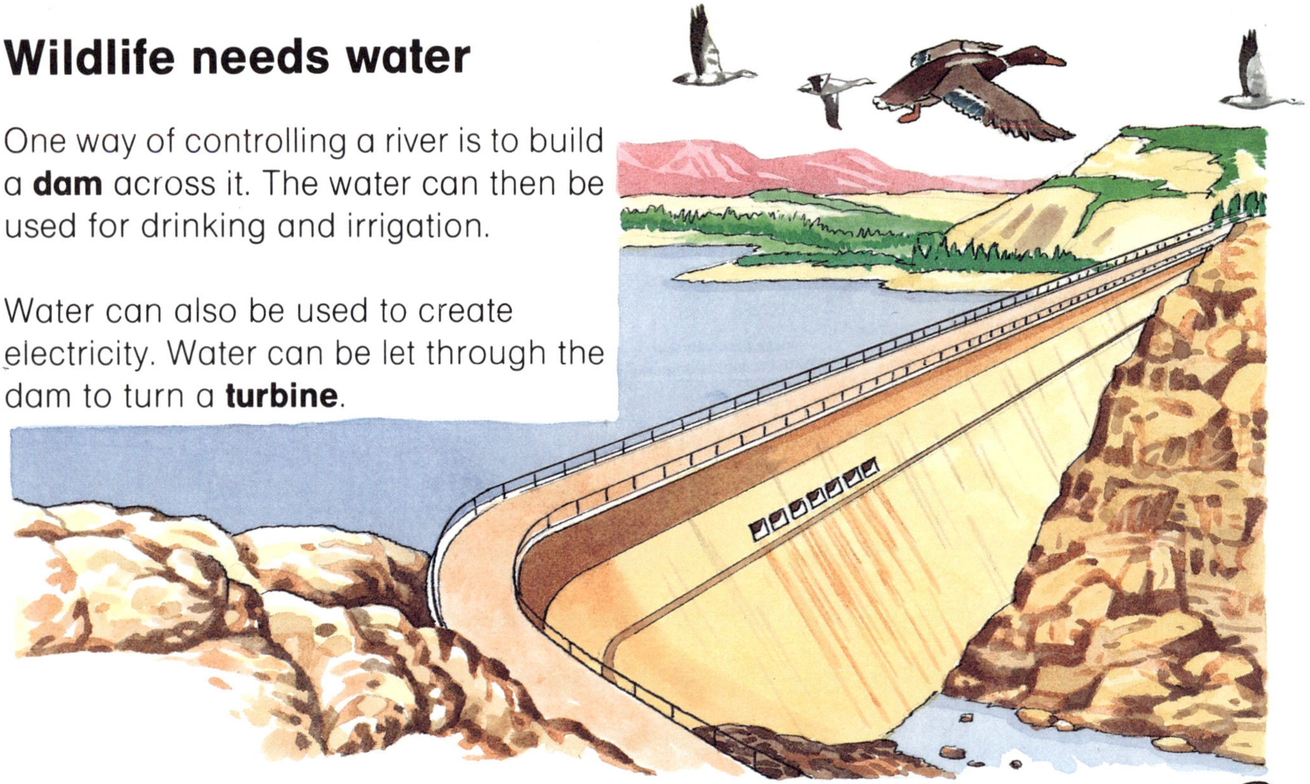

However, wildlife needs water as well as people. In Tunisia there is a **national park** called Ichkeul with a lake which in winter is home to thousands of geese and ducks.

Some people want to build dams across the rivers that flow into the lake. The lake is next to the sea but the rivers stop too much sea water from getting in.

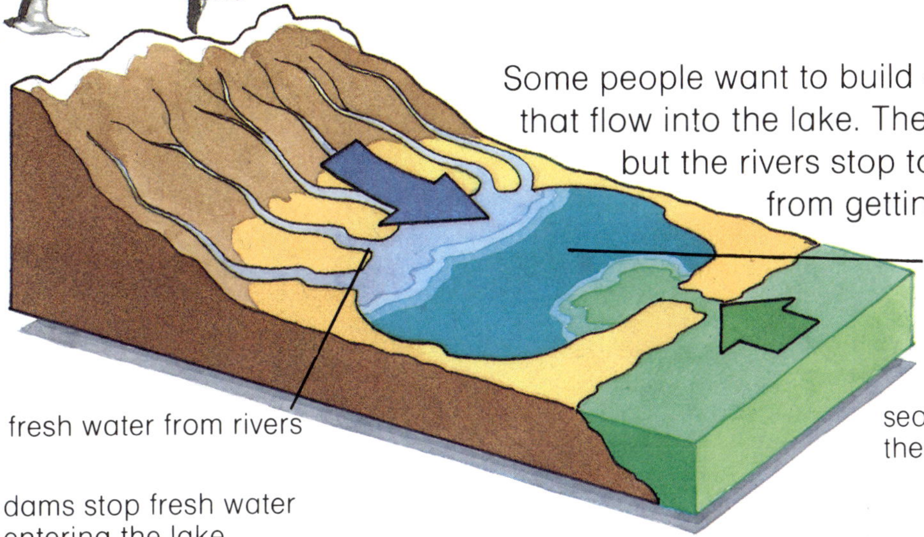


Once the dams are built there will be less fresh water flowing into the lake. The lake would become saltier. Plants and animals which are the food of ducks and geese would die because they cannot live in salty sea water.

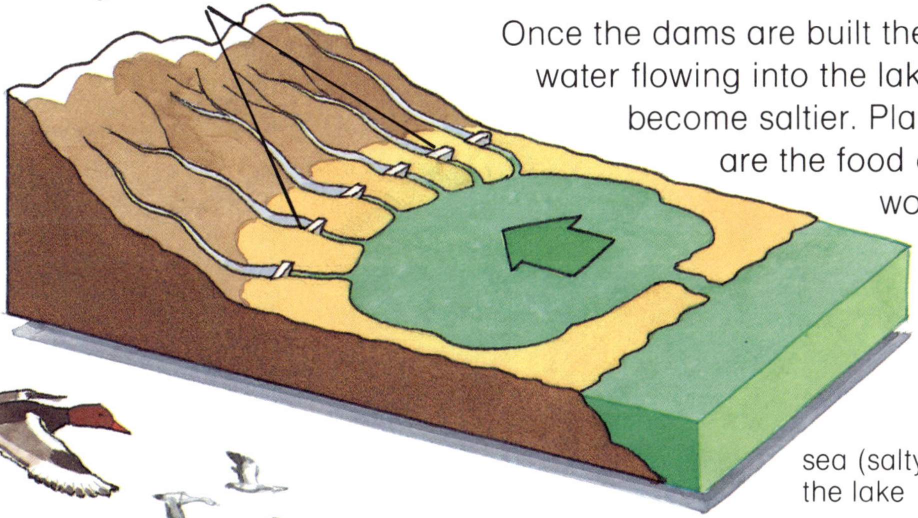


Fortunately, Ichkeul and its ducks and geese might be saved because there will be a sluice, a kind of gate between the sea water and the lake. This will help to stop the sea water getting in.

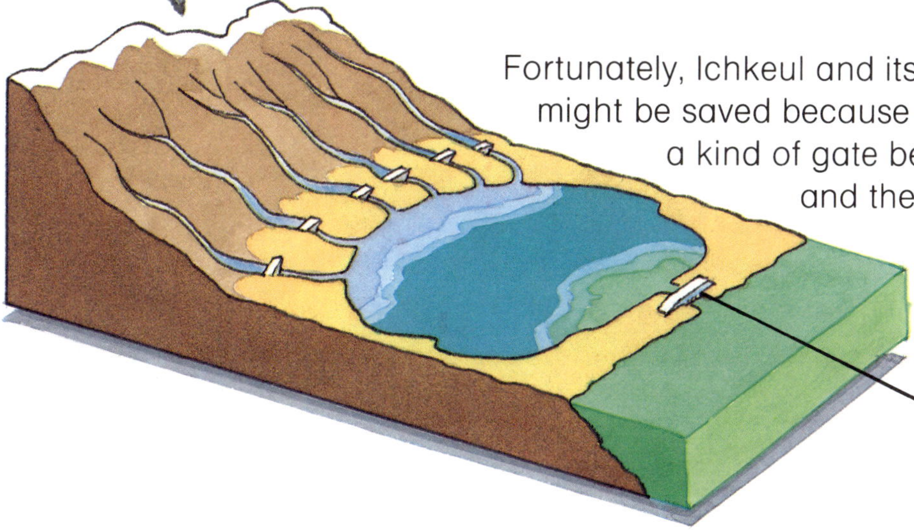

# At the seaside

A day at the seaside wherever you are in the world may not always be as pleasant as you hope. What can you see on this page which would make you think twice about swimming in the sea or staying on this beach? And if you look in the boxes you can see what's happening underwater and out at sea.

The fish looks annoyed with all the sewage and waste from the drain.

These gulls are eating polluted fish which is not good for them.

These ships have dumped rubbish and poisons in the sea.

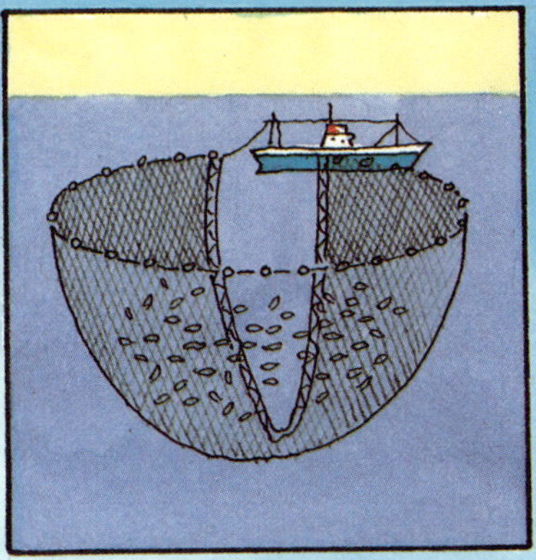

These fishing boats are bringing their catch back to shore.

All this pollution and rubbish only makes our lives unpleasant but worse still it can cause disease and can kill wildlife. Turn to the next page to find out about what might happen next.

# Taking more care

When we do not care about the environment, we create problems for ourselves and wildlife.

These problems need not happen. Today, more and more people care about what happens in their environment. Some of the problems are therefore being solved. Here are a few examples.

Polluted sea water made the boy sick.

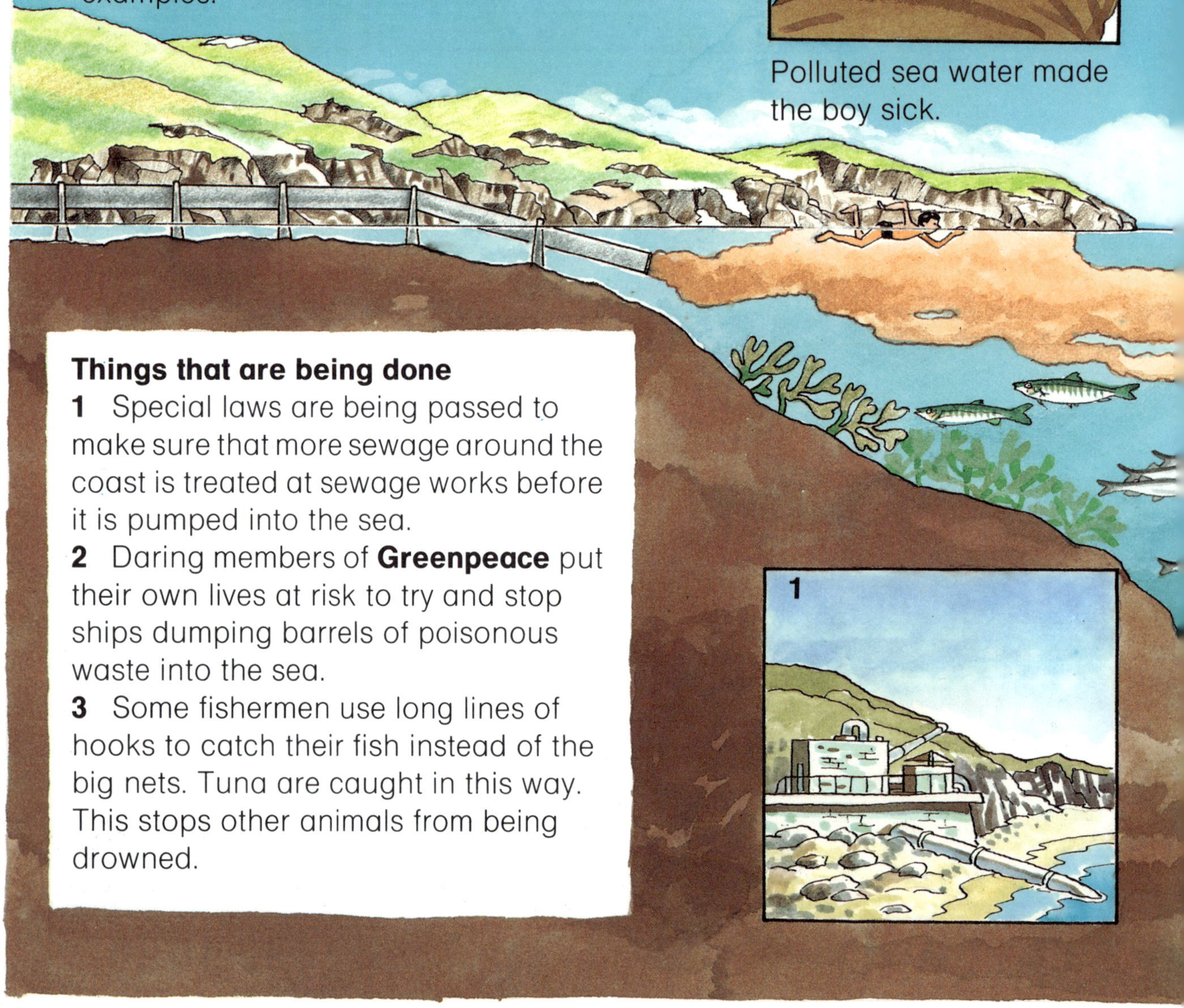

**Things that are being done**

**1** Special laws are being passed to make sure that more sewage around the coast is treated at sewage works before it is pumped into the sea.

**2** Daring members of **Greenpeace** put their own lives at risk to try and stop ships dumping barrels of poisonous waste into the sea.

**3** Some fishermen use long lines of hooks to catch their fish instead of the big nets. Tuna are caught in this way. This stops other animals from being drowned.

Poisonous chemicals have killed many fish and a seabird.

The nets which some fishing boats use also catch dolphins, seals and sea birds.

# Oil pollution

Huge **supertanker** ships move all over the oceans carrying oil. If they are damaged, their **cargo** of oil may spill into the sea. Oil spreads very quickly over water and it doesn't take long before much of the sea and coastline are covered in the thick, sticky crude oil. Sea birds are the first to die. When oil gets into the feathers of birds it stops them from working properly. The birds can't stay warm and die from the cold.

The same happens to some sea **mammals**. Sea otters only keep healthy when their fur is clean. Seals aren't so badly affected because they have a thick layer of **blubber** for protection.

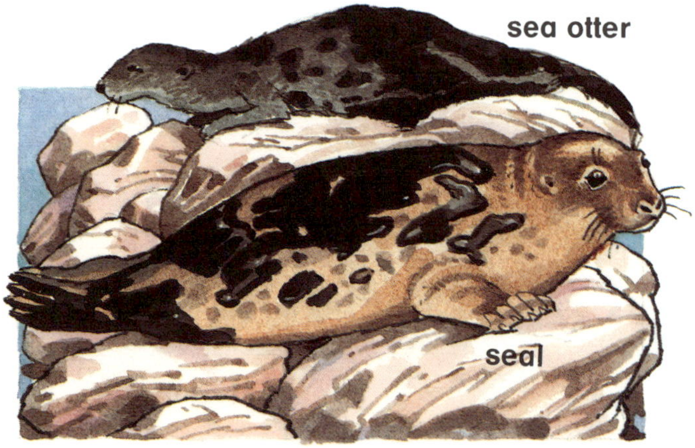

Other life under the sea is killed by the oil. Small animals such as clams, limpets, mussels and snails are **suffocated** by a thick blanket of oil. Animals may come to the shore-line to eat dead and dying fish. Oil can be poisonous too. Bears, the rare bald eagle and river otters see those fish as an easy meal. What might happen to them later? They may be poisoned too.

This happened recently in Alaska, in North America, where a huge oil spill killed many animals.

People clean oiled birds and sea otters.

The large plastic **booms** stop the oil from spreading.

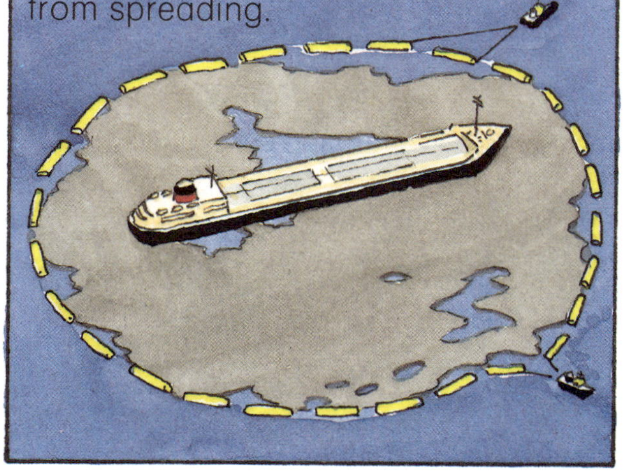

# Sea resources

For thousands of years people have hunted the oceans for fish and shellfish. Using old-fashioned methods such as spearing, hooks and lines, or nets thrown from small boats, they could only catch quite small numbers at a time. So in those days there was never a problem of overfishing.

In the early 1900s bigger boats were used to catch fish called herrings. They used nets with small holes which caught both big and small fish. After a few years there were hardly any herrings left. Because they caught all the small fish there were none left to grow into big fish.

## Fish farming

Sometimes we can farm fish rather than going out to catch them. We keep them in large tanks, feed them, breed them and then eat them for food. Only a few kinds of fish can be kept in this way. For example, a fish called tilapia in Africa and the rainbow trout in Europe.

# Using water wisely

The world's oceans occupy two-thirds of the Earth's surface. There is still so much to understand about the sea. One minute we are using it as a drain and the next playing in it. We **harvest** food and yet there are probably lots of other ways we could use it to help us. We can no longer go on pouring all the dangerous waste and materials into the sea and expect it to stay clean for us. Who knows what damage and disease we are causing to ourselves? The more we do the more it will harm us.

**Here are some ways we use the sea:**

In some countries shellfish such as mussels, oysters and clams are luxury foods. They are harvested along the coast and sold in restaurants.

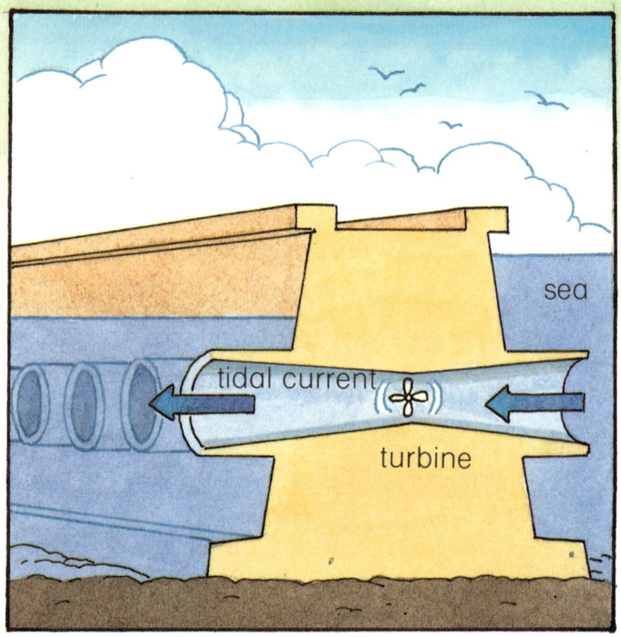


The motion of the waves and changes of the tides produce energy which we can use. Here is a machine which changes the movements of tides into electricity.

Deep on the sea-bed lie minerals, such as manganese, which are useful to us. These minerals are collected using a special machine.

For thousands of years the sea has provided people with a rich source of food.

The large seaweed called 'kelp' is farmed and harvested from the sea. It produces a chemical called **algin** which is used in industry.

Coral reefs are beautiful and precious. But they are in danger from people who are chipping away pieces to sell to tourists.

# How you can help

You can find out whether river water is clear or polluted by looking at what lives there. You will need a net. It is easy to make one from a net curtain, a wire coathanger and a pole. Strap the net onto the pole using hosepipe clips and tape. Using the net, collect samples from the river or pond bed. Put them in a white tray so you can see what is there. A magnifying glass will help you see the animals living there. Look at pages 10 and 11 to find out what lives in a stream or pond. Even better, look at page 30 which tells you where you can get more information to help you.

### A net

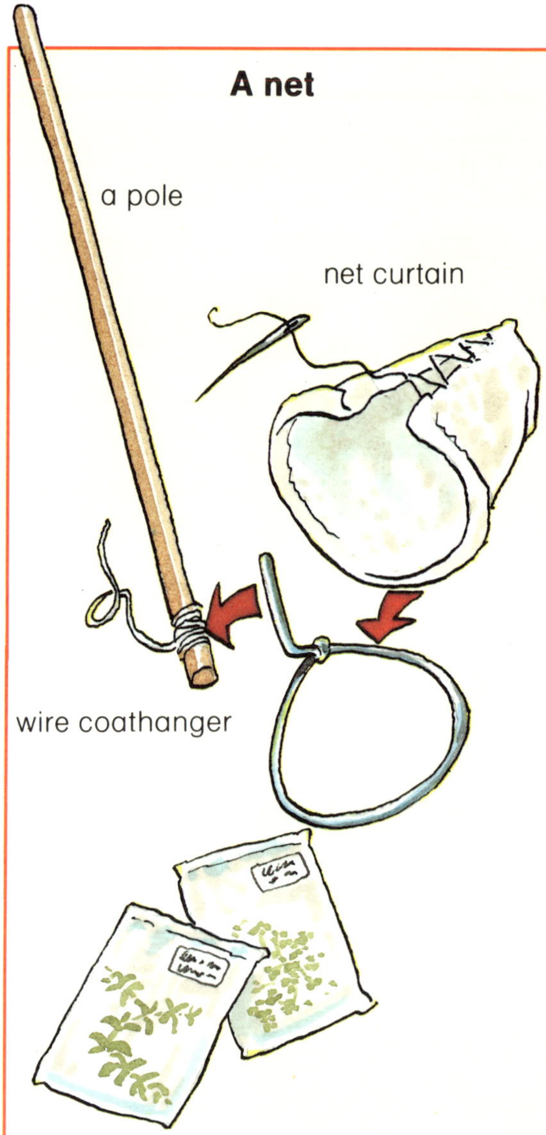


### Safety tips

- Never go near water which looks heavily polluted.
- Always have a grown-up with you.
- Wear rubber gloves and always wash your hands after handling water.
- Pick a safe part of the bank.

These days strolling along a beach can be messy. Watch out for tar, sewage outfalls and dangerous bits of rubbish. There can be a lot on some beaches. Where you see something nasty or where there is an unpleasant smell on the beach, tell the grown-up you are with. You may also find lots of interesting objects. On the left are just a few you might find. If you want to find living animals and plants, rockpools are the best place to look.

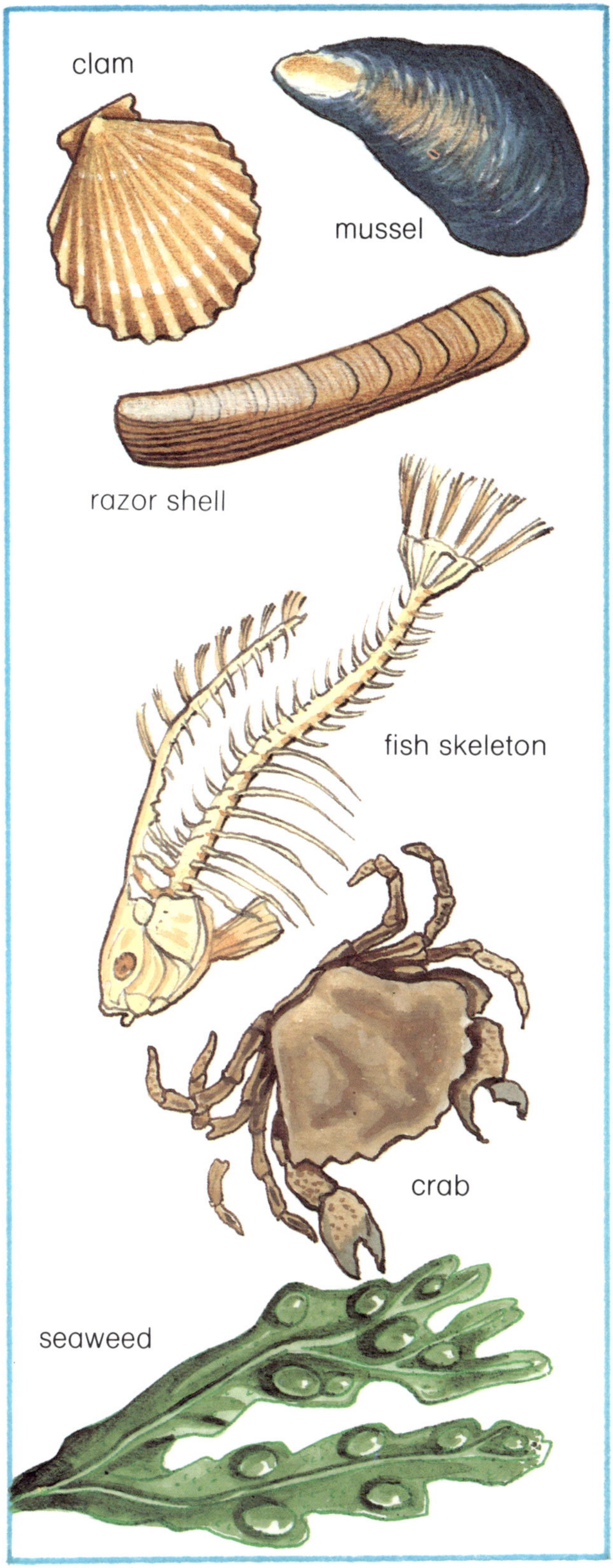

# Water fact file

### Spreading disease
When water becomes filled with human waste, then human diseases spread very quickly. Typhoid and cholera are fatal diseases which can be picked up in water. Four out of every five common diseases in developing countries are caused either by dirty water or lack of sanitation. It is estimated that there are about 25,000 deaths every day in the developing world caused by water-borne diseases.

### Frozen water
Less than 1% of the supply of fresh water is available for human use. The rest is locked away in glaciers and the Polar ice caps.

### The River Amazon
The River Amazon, in South America, carries more water than any other river in the world. In fact, it carries almost one sixth of all the water found in all the rivers on Earth.

### Wasted water
Irrigation, which accounts for the bulk of agricultural use, is very wasteful – often more than 70% of the water used for irrigation never reaches the crops.

### Cutting down forests
When forests are cut down, particularly tropical forests, there is no plant life to soak up the water like a sponge and let it out gradually. Without plants, water rushes down onto the soil and washes the soil away into rivers. This leaves the land barren and nothing can grow there.

### Using water
Just flushing a toilet requires 10 litres of water while a single shower uses nearer 100 litres of water.

### Fresh water
Fresh water is used for three main purposes: agriculture, industry, and domestic supply.

**Salty water**

More than 97% of the water on the Earth is sea-water.

**Water for life**

Pure water does not taste of anything; it does not smell of anything; and is colourless when found in small quantities. It is the most common liquid on earth. It is made from hydrogen and oxygen (its chemical formula is $H_2O$). It is very important for all living animals and plants. In fact, nothing could live if all the water on Earth was taken away. People would quickly die if they could not find water to drink.

**Life from water**

Many scientists believe that life on Earth began in the seas and oceans millions of years ago.

**Without water**

At least 1,700 million people do not have an adequate supply of drinking water and some 3,000 million are without proper sanitation.

# Further information

There are many organisations involved with helping nature and our environment. Below are the addresses of just some of the more well known ones that you may like to contact. They may also be able to put you in touch with local organisations, if you want to get actively involved with things such as fund-raising through sponsored events. Remember, our natural world needs every friend and helper it can get!

Friends of the Earth
26-28 Underwood Street
London N1 7JQ

World Wide Fund for Nature
Panda House
Weyside Park
Godalming
Surrey GU7 1XR

British Trust for Nature Conservation Volunteers
36 St Mary's Street
Wallingford
Oxfordshire OX10 0EU

Greenpeace
30-31 Islington Green
London N1 8XT

The Conservation Trust
George Palmer Site
Northumberland Avenue
Reading
Berkshire RG2 7PW

Royal Society for the Protection of Birds
The Lodge
Sandy
Bedfordshire

The People's Trust for Endangered Species
Hamble House
Meadrow
Godalming
Surrey GU7 3JX

# Glossary

**Acid rain** Rain that is mixed with polluting chemicals. It makes a weak acid and is harmful to plants and animals.

**Algin** An edible gum that comes from seaweed, used to thicken some soups and jellies. It is also used in the textile industry.

**Blubber** A thick, fatty layer found just under the outer surface of the skin in many sea animals, such as whales.

**Boom** A plastic floating barrier used when controlling an oil spill.

**Cargo** The goods carried by a ship or similar vessel.

**Dam** A barrier built across a river to slow or stop the flow of water.

**Evaporate** To turn into steam or vapour, usually by heating a liquid, such as water.

**Greenpeace** An international charitable organisation that helps protect the environment and our wildlife from harm.

**Harvest** The produce or crop collected by people, usually for eating or drinking.

**Mammals** Warm-blooded animals that feed their young on milk from the mother's breast.

**National park** An area of land that is set aside for wild animals, birds, plants and trees.

**Nitrates** A fertilizer used by farmers to help grow more crops on their land.

**Oxygen** A colourless gas, without taste or smell. It is found in the air and water and is important to all living things.

**Reservoir** A lake made by people in which to store water.

**Sewage system** Sewage is the waste created by people. It is carried away in sewers to a place where it is cleaned. This is the sewage system.

**Suffocate** Making a person or animal or plant unable to breathe.

**Supertanker** A very large ship that is designed to carry huge quantities of oil from one part of the world to another.

**Turbine** A motor with blades (like those of a windmill). It is driven by water falling onto the blades.

**Well** A natural or man-made source of fresh drinking water. Often a well is dug deep into the earth to reach a source of clear water suitable for people to drink.

# Index